Sequoya's Daily Inspiration

Volume I

By

Sequoya Ylett Trimble

Copyright © 2020 Sequoya Ylett Trimble

All rights reserved. No part of this publication may be reproduced, distributed, or transmitted in any form or by any means, including photocopying, recording, or other electronic or mechanical methods, without the prior written permission of the publisher, except in the case of brief quotations embodied in critical reviews and certain other noncommercial uses permitted by copyright law.

ISBN-13: 978-19513002-0-3

Liberation's Publishing LLC ~ West Point, Mississippi

Dedication

This book is dedicated to: my Grandparents Joe and Mary Trimble that inspire, motivate, and continue to support me in life, my Mother Connie Whitfield which she taught me about Christ at an early age, and she pushed me to accomplish anything I set my mind to, my son Seth Dennie that changed my life forever and loves me unconditionally daily, all nine of my siblings especially Saprina Jones, you have always encouraged and inspired me to soar like an eagle since I was a little girl and presently, my friends especially Trish Hubbard we may be far away, but you're always here and thinking of me, my past & present relationships, and failures in life. A special thanks to my Prophet Ali and Gosale Yesu Kantarzis from Ghana, you have prayed continuously with me & for me, spoke blessings into my life, covered me, and constantly remind me what thus said the Lord. The number one dedication goes out to my Lord and Savior Jesus Christ none of this would be possible without you. I love you all dearly.

Day 1

Don't let the D's get you down. FIGHT: The "Devil" will try to "Distract" you to make you feel like the "Devastation" will cause "Destruction" in your life forever. BUT the Devil is a liar, and no weapon formed against you shall prosper. God can heal any situation.

Day 2

You may feel like everything keeps going wrong and nothing is going right. One might ask the question, "What did I do or why do I have to go through all of this?" Just know you were "chosen." So, why not you? It's a process, and the drought won't last forever. Stay steadfast, your blessing is near.

Day 3

Have you ever thought about the reason you can't find a job? Maybe it's because God didn't intend for you to work for someone else, but for yourself. How can someone be your boss when there's a boss within you? Be your own "BOSS."

You are destined to be a leader.

Day 4

Believers don't say "but". Saying "but" distracts from your goals, your dreams, and your destination. Do you believe? If you do, don't say "but". Saying "but" distracts you from your goal, your dream, and your destination. But is saying forget everything you believe.

 Day 5

Stop listening to others. Everyone has an opinion regarding what they think you should do. Only God knows the answer. Ask God. Stop seeking the approval of others.

Day 6

True peace comes from following the plan God has for you. Attempting to live outside of God's will, leads to chaos and uncertainty. No matter what you try to do in life, you won't be at peace until you do what God has called you to do.

What is your heart's desire? Don't do something just to be doing it. If you do it, ensure you're passionate about it.

Let us not worry because of current circumstances but let us rejoice because our now doesn't determine our future. The battle is already won.

Day 9

Move on and forgive those who hurt you. Don't miss out on your blessings because someone hurt you. Learn to forgive and move forward. Forgiveness is a daily process of asking God to help you forgive.

Day 10

Just because you haven't accomplished your goals doesn't mean you should give up. Some of the most successful individuals were failures at first.

Day 11

Don't worry about what people say about you. Most of them look up to you, but they won't tell you. People secretly look up to you. You don't know they are watching and listening. You may not know this side of heaven who you're impacting.

Day 12

Sometime when all hell breaks loose, it's because your breakthrough is near or here. Stay focused! Don't give up! You've come too far.

Never compromise. Don't do anything that's not right. If you feel it's wrong, walk away and thank God for your instincts.

Day 14

If he or she left you, it's because God had something better for you. God knew that person wouldn't leave. So, He had to force him or her to leave you. Celebrate, rejoice, and be glad they are gone.

Day 15

Our kids are one of our greatest accomplishments. We must be thankful that God trusted us with our child(ren).

Day 16

"For my thoughts are not your thoughts, neither are your ways," declares the Lord. "As the heavens are higher than the earth, so are my ways higher than your ways and my thoughts than your thoughts."

Isaiah 55:8-9 (KJV)

Day 17

Make sure you learn from every mistake in life. Don't wallow in regret - learn and grow from your mistakes.

Day 18

Don't compare yourself to others because they appear to have it together. You don't see their struggles. They are living in debt because of the nice things they own. What you see is not always what it appears to be. Be careful what you wish for.

Day 19

If we can be sold out for our favorite sports team, we can be sold out for the Lord and some more. Let's give God the praises daily like we praise our favorite team daily. God's team is the best team ever. Support Him and be the winner He created you to be.

No one is perfect. If we were, we wouldn't need the Lord.

Day 21

Your season isn't your neighbor's season. "Oh ye of a little faith." God has a time, a reason, and a season just for you. So be patient.

Day 22

Rejection, failure, and loss is not bad. Through it all you will gain what God truly has for you.

Learn to celebrate when it happens.

Day 23

Don't worry about who's talking about you or watching you. Just keep praising God. The ones watching and talking want what you have.

Day 24

So, what? You messed up! Don't stop trying to do the right thing. Keep trying over & over again. The one time you decide to quit trying might be the last chance you get to try.

Day 25

Be aware of the negative other half - friends, family members, associates, or co-workers speaking negative things over you. If an individual can't deposit positive things into your life, let them go. You need someone to build you up, not tear you down.

Day 26

You don't need 10,000 people following you to do what God has called you to do. Isolation is good, and it's ok if you only deal with two. Separation is required for where God is taking you.

Day 27

"The Lord bless thee and keep thee: The Lord make His face shine upon thee and be gracious unto thee: The Lord lift up His countenance upon thee, and give the peace."
Numbers 6:24-26 (KJV)

You don't need anyone to believe in you. Just believe in yourself and know that God believes in you.

Day 29

For many years, we have been testing the fire while we live without a purpose. We've been doing things our way because we're just living to live. When in all actuality, we're crying out for help, and this leads to looking for love in all the wrong places.

Day 30

"For God hath not given us the spirit of fear; but of power, and of love, and of a sound mind." 2 Timothy 1:7 (KJV)

Day 31

Your setback is just preparing you for your setup. Greater is coming.

What's your passion? Make sure you're doing what makes you happy in life.

Instead of complaining about adversity, think about all the good things that will and can come from it.

Day 34

If people didn't hate you or hate on you, you wouldn't have anyone to help challenge your GROWTH. Haters serve a purpose in life. So, keep them around.

Life can be ugly or beautiful. Which one do you choose? Life is what you make out of it.

Day 36

No matter what it looks like, feels like, or seems like you still pursue it; until you get it.

You never need man's approval, but you do need the Lord's approval.

Day 38

It does not matter what you did yesterday or yesteryear. Start over and change. God still loves you. It's not too late to change.

Day 39

If anything comes against you make sure you bind the devil and plead the blood of Jesus over your situation. There's POWER in the name of Jesus.

Day 40

Get a grip on it! There's someone going through a lot more than you or worse. You better be thankful and stop complaining.

Day 41

For many years we have done things our way. Now, it's time to let go and let God fully direct our path. Your direction lies within Him. Ask God what's next.

Day 42

Be careful who you follow because some family, friends, co-workers, significant others, and crowds specialize in leading people to HELL. Follow JESUS. He's the only one that can get you into HEAVEN.

Give thanks for your past, present, and future. God is good, and we must be thankful for everything. THANK YOU JESUS!

Day 44

When you find yourself in the same situation over and over again, it's something you're not doing right. You need to let go, change your life, and pass the test. When you're sick and tired of being sick and tired, you have no choice but to change.

Day 45

The things that keep tripping you up in life, God will deliver you in the middle of it, and give you a testimony to share and help others with.

No one wants to make mistakes in life but know that through your mistakes you're being MADE and GROWING into the man/woman of God you are destined to be.

When you don't get what you want, just know God is looking out for you. After all, He knows the number of hairs on your head and what's best in your interest.

Day 48

Don't wait on your family, friends, or community to promote you or support you. God will send new supporters and followers along the way. You don't need man to promote you because God does all the demoting and promoting anyway.

Day 49

Sometimes we get so busy chasing success, money, businesses, and tangible things, we forget God gives us those things. If we chase God instead of all those things, everything will automatically come. You don't have to chase what God already has for you.

Day 50

When you have no idea how God is going to do it, just continue to trust Him. God is going to make a way out of no way. God is saying, "Trust Me."

Day 51

We have all done sinned. Don't let your past keep you from reaching your future. God forgives us even when we don't forgive ourselves.

Day 52

Do you want to change? First, you must be dissatisfied and determined to change. You don't have to go another day being dissatisfied. You have the power to do something about it.

Day 53

You have talked about it long enough. Now what are you going to do about it? Don't focus on your problem without also focusing on a solution.

Day 54

It's ok to be different & not normal because normal isn't normal.

Day 55

We know what God can do. So, when life changes or throws you a curve ball you got to keep the faith.

Day 56

If every block falls down, and you're unable to determine the structure you're building, take each block and start building something else again. It always happens, just when you thought you had it all together, something will interrupt you. God knows you can complete the job. Even when we don't think we can.

Day 57

You don't have to be perfect, but you can strive daily to be the best version of you. Every day strive to do better than the day before.

Day 58

Create a business or invention no one else has. Think about something that no other individual has invented. Be creative and different. Then God will limit your competition. You won't have to worry about your competitors.

Day 59

If he or she can't stimulate your heart, mind, and soul spiritually then they are not the one for you. You need a mate who will help you grow and get you to the next level in Christ. Be careful who you are attracting, and make sure he/she knows how to love you. What is your foundation based on? What's turning you on?

If we can't manage the small things God gives us and be obedient & faithful with them, how can God trust us with more?

Day 61

In the most painful times silence is the best solution. Don't speak because they're waiting to see how you will react. Let your actions speak for you instead.

Day 62

In the most unclear & uncertain areas in your life find HOPE from within. Keep going during times of despair.

Day 63

Today is a new day and the beginning of a new week. Let's make the best out of it. What will you do different this day and week?

Day 64

If you're reading this, you have been given another chance to do something you didn't do yesterday. Take advantage of this day and hour.

Day 65

When everything goes wrong, keep the faith. We might not know how, when, or where, but trust God. He always makes a way. He will never forsake you.

Day 66

Today is a new day – you have been given another opportunity to make a difference; therefore, change and make a difference today. Don't put things off for tomorrow when you can do it today - tomorrow isn't promised.

Day 67

God will keep us in His hand. In every moment God will cover us, and He will not fail us.

You don't have to chase something that's already yours; it will come running to you.

We all have a gift from God. What are we doing with our gifts? Are we keeping them for ourselves?

Everything you do in life is an appointment for your future.

Day 71

When you hear or see someone acting out of their character, don't worry. They are not acting – you are seeing their true character. Their mask hides their true character.

-What individuals display at work and church isn't always who they really are.

Day 72

You may do something for someone then never hear from them again, until the next time they build up courage to ask you for something else.

If you're inspired to do something, do it. Don't let any man talk you out of it. If you're thinking it, I'm sure someone else is too.

Day 74

Confession is good for the soul. We can't change what we did yesterday or yesteryear, but we can ask for forgiveness, forgive ourselves, and move forward. Make a difference today and the days to come. Stop living in the past.

Day 75

Take a deep breath and breathe again. Now refocus and find your balance. Can you see the light now?

Just because you don't see it in the natural doesn't mean God hasn't worked it out in the spiritual. We must believe it before we see it.

Day 77

We all have to start somewhere. Just be willing to do it or go when asked.

Day 78

You don't have to worry because God has already taken care of it.

Day 79

Distractions will come to attack and distract you. Be watchful and aware of people's intentions. Everybody is not for you.

Day 80

Don't allow the distractions, negativity and destruction keep you from moving forward. This too shall pass.

"Give thanks to the Lord, for He is good; His love endures forever." Psalms 107:1 ((KJV)

Day 82

God will expose all things. People can no longer hide because what lies deep within us will eventually come to light.

Day 83

What God has for you, is for you. The devil in hell cannot stop you or take anything away from you that God hasn't ordained. Remember Job? God restored everything the devil stole. Be blessed and be of good cheer amid your trials.

Day 84

Man has created a delusion that life is free of problems and issues because many only share the good and hide the bad. Be honest about your situation, instead of creating a false reality for others to see.

Day 85

In this life, people aren't held accountable for their wrongdoings. We are living in a society where man views right as wrong and wrong as right. Somehow, we forget right is right and wrong is wrong.

Day 86

Life is beautiful - enjoy it! Live, love, and laugh today.

Day 87

Don't do it for people, do it for God and yourself.

Day 88

You may not be where others are, but God still loves you and cares. Your relationship with God and your life matters just like anyone else's. Don't let others belittle you and put you down.

Day 89

Change your environment and you can change your life. PEACE!!!

Let's fix our own lives before we try to fix someone else's life.

Day 91

Be happy and thankful! Live life with a smile on your face no matter what. Don't let others rob you of your joy & peace.

Day 92

Just because things didn't go as planned doesn't mean you should give up. Keep going!!!

You can be irrelevant to everyone in the world, but please remember you're relevant to GOD.

Day 94

You don't need a thousand individuals to believe in you. It only takes one person, and you.

Day 95

It's easy for some to pretend to care about you. They are in your life because they feel they have to be, not because they want to be. Identify who's real and who's fake. Everybody is not for you just because they say they're for you. Know who's really on your team.

Day 96

Give because you're a cheerful giver, not because you're looking for something in return.

Live and Love life with no regrets. Be of good cheer.

God has given us the tools and resources to start and finish our tasks. Are we utilizing our resources and tools?

Day 99

You are a blessing, and God loves you. Love yourself. God loves you even when you don't feel like others love you. Remember God is love.

Day 100

Today is a new day. Don't let yesteryear or yesterday stop you from making a difference today.

Day 101

There's a reason for every season. Don't create a season or make up a reason.

Day 102

Let's not make decisions for our personal gratification and because of our human error. Let's make decisions based on doing the right thing, even when doing the right thing can be difficult. Doing what's right is the Right Thing to Do.

Day 103

Life goes on, but don't let it go on without you.

Day 104

It doesn't matter how much money you make or have. It can't replace a life. It may attempt to fill a void, but it will never replace the loss.

Day 105

Some of the things we thought were important in life aren't important anymore.

Even if all the items appear to be taken, don't give up. God has a special item just for you.

Day 107

It doesn't matter who writes you off. As long as you're in God's hands, nothing is impossible.

Day 108

Be careful who and what you surround yourself with because eventually you will start displaying whatever they're displaying.

Day 109

We must face the things we have ran from. Stop running and face the things you are running from.

Day 110

Daily we have an opportunity for growth. So, don't let another day go by without taking advantage of the opportunity.

Day 111

Happiness does exist, but what are we doing to obtain it?

Day 112

When everyone keeps telling you the same thing over and over again, you might want to listen.

Sometimes we are so concerned about others that we neglect ourselves.

Day 114

Be patient and know it will all come together. For every heartache, setback, and delay you have gone through God is going to restore and bless you.

Day 115

When you're going through be thankful and praise God in the middle of your storm because your breakthrough is near. Praise Him before, during, and after the storm.

Day 116

Life events cause change. Whether the outcome is positive or negative, how you respond to that change is up to you. Follow the path of positivity.

Day 117

We must be content in our current situation, but don't be content where you're not willing to change, grow, and increase in any situation.

Day 118

Chin up and head high and make sure you walk with confidence. It's not over.

Day 119

If you're still alive, that's important. Rejoice because you're still fulfilling your purpose.

It doesn't matter who or what they call you. It matters what you answer to.

Success is determined by the individual.
Everyone won't see your success as success.

Day 122

Procrastination can keep you from reaching your goals and it causes you to become content when you're capable of accomplishing more.

Day 123

Pain can either continue to hurt you or motivate you.

Day 124

God's love is the best love. Learn how to love yourself and God before trying to love someone else.

Day 125

If people are speaking negative things about you continue to speak positive things about yourself. People will try to ruin your credibility.

Day 126

Your smile can make a difference in someone's life. You never know who's watching you. So, smile.

Day 127

Every man and woman has a gift within them, but if you're not willing to use your gift appropriately eventually God will give it to someone that will.

If you don't believe in yourself who will?

Keep on keeping on, no matter what.

Day 130

You failed? So, what! Some people take longer than others to get where they're going in life. It doesn't matter as long as you reach you destination. Stop watching the clock. Every second is a new opportunity to try again.

Day 131

If we gave up every time something goes wrong, we wouldn't have a productive life. So, turn the negative outcomes into positive opportunities.

Day 132

How can you say, "I want to be successful" if you're afraid to fail?

Day 133

Some of the most successful individuals were failures first. They failed many times before reaching a successful outcome.

Day 134

Anybody can find somebody, but it's about finding the right somebody. Be patient and wait for your mate.

Day 135

Our plans are not God's plans for our life. No matter what you want in life or think you should be doing you must be obedient and listen to the Lord. If God says "NO" then that's a NO! Don't question it.

Day 136

No matter what it feels like, seems like, or looks like we must praise God and be thankful. There is a time, reason, and season for everything.

Day 137

God will allow you to see things for what they are. So you don't be disturbed when it happens again.

Day 138

We should be excited for others and rejoice with them in the middle of their season of blessings. It's a beautiful thing!

Day 139

Find someone to help pull you up when you're down. Everyone needs someone positive in their life.

Day 140

There's a time for everything. Your time won't be the next person's time. Learn to continue to have great expectations even in the middle of your adversities.

Day 141

You don't have to be perfect, look like a star, talk perfect, have a clean past, be liked by many, or have supporters in order for God to use you. He wants someone that's willing. (I've learned) we can be so caught up in pleasing others, making them happy, or caught up in personal satisfaction that we miss the path or direction God is trying to take us. Please know, no matter the situation, it's never too late as long as you're alive. Don't let men tell you what you can and can't do. Lives are at stake; it's time. You messed up? So what! No one is perfect and can't no man walk this earth (but God) and say out of 365 days out of a year, "I did no wrong." The only perfect man to walk this earth was Jesus. No other man can say, "I've done no wrong". Continue to strive daily to walk Christ-like and strive for perfection. We are chasing the wrong things in life. It's time out for playing. In order to go to the next level, we will have to make sacrifices, leave some people behind, and be willing to be isolated. God has great things in store for you. GO GET IT!

Day 142

If we don't hold people accountable who will? If we let someone continue to get away with doing wrong, how would the individual ever have a desire to do what's right?

Day 143

Look how God blesses us with a gift or gifts after Christmas. Now the question is what are we going to do with all of our gifts? God has given each of us a spiritual gift as well, and some of us use it daily and some of us treat our gift like a Christmas gift. We open it, become excited about it, and use it for a little bit, but then we put it away. God is trying to bring out the best in us so we can be a huge gift to the body of Christ. Please don't put your gift on the shelf but use it or allow your gift to bless someone. God is good to us. He didn't have to even give us a gift, but He did. Let's use it!!

Day 144

Believe the impossible, see the vision, trust your mission, accomplish your goals, move forward, and act on your dream. Don't worry about what it looks like, feels like, or seems like. Just keep believing. God will send you all the support you need.

Day 145

Go look in the mirror, and there's your PROBLEM. Do you see it?

Day 146

Everyone has a time, reason, and season in your life. Identify their time, reason, and season. Make sure you ask the Lord, What's their purpose in my life?

Day 147

Don't let the world get the best of you. Sometimes we give a lot, pouring out our gifts and blessings to others. Make sure you acknowledge yourself and give to yourself before you give all of you to others.

Separation brings about isolation. Isolation is part of your season of growth.

Day 149

Just because you made a mistake doesn't mean it's over. Just because you're not where you want to be doesn't mean it's over. Just because you're hurting doesn't mean it's over. God wants to correct you, take you places, and heal you. Find strength within the Lord not man. Stop following people and trust the Lord. It's not over.

Day 150

God will use your kids to encourage us, warn us, and bless us. Take time out of your busy schedule to see what your child(ren) is trying to say.

Day 151

Be aware of church members that will show love to you in church but won't show love outside the church. Sometimes the church is hurting, but don't allow it to affect your praise. Pray and keep going.

Day 152

Every day won't be easy, and it will be a fight between your spirit man & yourself daily. Speak life over yourself, bind the devil, and know no weapon formed against you shall prosper.

Day 153

When everyone turns their back on you don't stop trusting the Lord. God will place people in your life to help you get to the next level. Don't be so caught up with who's not in your life. Remember, when times are hard and you feel alone, continue to trust the Lord.

Day 154

Family can be your worst enemy sometimes. They may turn on you, talk about you, and treat you with disrespect. When they do, show love and pray peace over them.

Day 155

You are who God says you are. You're a mighty man or woman of God. You're a blessing coming in and going out. No matter what it looks like you will prevail. Praise God in advance.

Day 156

No one is perfect, but you can strive daily to be Christ like. Don't allow man to talk you into not serving God, trusting, & praising Him. It's through our trials that God can deliver us and make us whole.

Day 157

Don't let anyone tell you your vision doesn't make sense. It won't make sense to the individual it's not given to.

Day 158

Christmas may be over, but Christ continues to live daily. He will never be over. So, let's continue to celebrate CHRIST every day.

Day 159

Speak affirmations over your situation, and know your breakthrough is near. Tell the devil it's time to reap what you have sown.

Man will be quick to discuss your errors, but you won't hear them discuss theirs.

Day 161

Start your day with great expectations. Today is a new day. Make the best out of it.

Day 162

Everything might appear to be at a standstill but be of good cheer. God is still near. He hasn't forgotten you.

Day 163

People talk a good game, but they have issues demonstrating what they talk about. Talk is cheap, actions tell a story.

Day 164

Let's be patient if we're single. Anybody can find somebody, but it's about finding the right somebody. Be thankful it didn't work. She/he wasn't the one anyway. Thank God for His intervening. Would you rather be single or taken & miserable? Let's enjoy life, and when he/she comes we can continue to enjoy life with them. It makes no sense being single and unhappy. God has destined someone for you. Be vigilant in your wait. Use the time to work on yourself. You might as well make the best out of it.

Don't let anyone look down on you. They too have a past & present.

Day 166

Give thanks to the Lord. God has been good to us, and we must thank Him daily for our life, the people in it, and the people no longer in our life.

Day 167

There's a battle going on. The enemy is trying to devour us, but he can't conquer and win, unless you forfeit the fight.

Day 168

We all have goals, but are we accomplishing them? Write down the vision and making it plain and clear. Place your vision as a daily reminder of the thing(s) you are striving for.

Day 169

As we all battle with something, we see a loss or win at the end, but it doesn't matter if you lose or win. What really matters is what you did during the battle. That's what counts. It tells if we fought the battle or not.

Day 170

If you're off track, you still have time to make a difference, but don't focus on the year. Take every day serious and one day at a time. If you fail, get back up and keep trying, but don't keep taking advantage of each day because tomorrow isn't promised.

Day 171

Whatever doesn't serve your purpose in life, just let it go. Let go of the things that prevent you from living out your purpose. Those things hinder your growth.

Day 172

Speak to yourself and your situation, trust God, believe, decree, and declare it. And so, shall it be.

When you don't know which way to go, keep going and ask God to direct your path.

Day 174

You don't have to see it to believe it. Just keep believing it. That's FAITH!

With God on your side, you will not lack anything. Stop worrying about how, and just know He's going to do it.

Day 176

Some things can't be avoided in life;
therefore, you will face tomorrow.

Day 177

Whatever your passion is make sure it's your occupation.

Day 178

Motivation, determination, and inspiration keeps you going in life.

Day 179

Some people will never understand that God didn't intend for them only to be successful, blessed, and accomplished in life. God wants all of us to be blessed and saved. Stop thinking the world revolves around you. You're not the only person God is directing and blessing.

Day 180

Support one another in life, and if you want support make sure you're giving support to others.

Day 181

Don't force it. Some things were not meant to work. It's supposed to remain broke. Stop trying to fix it. Thank God and move forward.

Day 182

Satisfaction is determined by the individual. What satisfies one might not satisfy the next individual.

Day 183

A lot of things we miss due to a lack of knowledge, but wouldn't it be reasonable if people would inform others? Be informative and help & bless others! You didn't get this far in life on your own. Somebody helped you.

Day 184

Reach your full potential. Don't stop where you are in life.

Day 185

If we settle, how will we experience the true blessings God has for us just because we won't be patient and wait on the Lord?

Day 186

Just Keep Going!!!

Day 187

There will be days you won't feel like going on, but you must trust GOD and continue to move forward in life.

Day 188

People will try to bring you down and destroy your name but remember man didn't make you and they can't take who you are away from you.

Day 189

Don't let no man or woman make you feel you're not valuable because you are. God made each of us and he has a purpose just for you.

Day 190

No weapon formed against you shall proposer. God didn't say it wouldn't form, but He did say it wouldn't proposer.

Day 191

You may feel like you're at a standstill in life, but God has you right where He wants you. You're being made and it's just part of the process. So, be still.

Day 192

Family, friends, your spouse, significant other, co-workers, and the world might turn against you, but know God will never turn against you. Trust Him and not man.

The blood of Jesus covers you and by Jesus' stripes you are healed.

Day 194

You don't have to see it before you believe it.
Even in the midst of you not understanding,
continue to TRUST GOD.

Day 195

When you can't go to the left, right, look up or down, or call anyone, just call on the name of Jesus. Tell Him all about your troubles.

If you can't say anything nice today, don't say anything at all. Just smile and keep going.

Day 197

Today, you may face trials and tribulations, but you must call on the name of Jesus to help you get through this day.

Day 198

Everyone won't support you and show you love. Make sure you support and love yourself.

Day 199

Don't let your life be influenced by money because money comes and go. Find something to make you thrive in life besides money.

Day 200

Not everybody cares if you make it. Make sure you got the right people on your team because everybody is not cheering for you on your team.

Day 201

You don't have to be bitter and negative because people around you are bitter and negative. Smile and stay positive during all situation.

Day 202

Don't live life to be liked. Exemplify your uniqueness. You were not made to be like others. Being different is a good thing.

Your plans can deviate at any minute. Don't be afraid to change at any time.

Day 204

You might have plenty problems, but God is the solution to all of your problems. We trust everyone else with our problems and issues, so why is it so hard to trust the Lord?

Day 205

Don't let anyone distract you and keep you from your goals.

You don't have to apologize for your success because it wasn't accomplished by anybody, but you.

Day 207

Every day will not be easy, but remember daily who and what you're living for, so you can keep going.

Don't let your past keep you from your future because your past won't determine your future unless you let it.

Day 209

Love covers a multitude. So, show man nothing, but love.

Day 210

You didn't have to grow up with the best childhood to live the best life.

Day 211

Sometimes we allow our past to dictate our future when our past has no control over our future.

Day 212

Be careful what you're wishing for while you're on the outside looking in. You don't know the struggle one is going through on the inside.

If someone is interested in you, they will show interest in you.

Day 214

God wants us to be blessed, and we should want to see others blessed as well. If it's anything you want to accomplish in life keep trying even if you can't see the progress. Eventually, your breakthrough will come.

Day 215

When people put you down, just know God will always push you up. Stay encouraged! You can do anything you put your mind to.

Day 216

People will never tell you, but they're watching you. Be careful what you do and say because people are watching you. You may be the only Bible they see.

Day 217

You will meet different people in life but only a few will stand out. The ones that were very rude and kind usually stand out. People will remember how you treated them. If it was a bad experience most likely they won't forget.

Day 218

Don't worry about what people say because they can't get you into heaven. They can lead you to hell, but it's up to you to get yourself into heaven.

Day 219

Sometimes we forget we haven't always had it all together; therefore, we forget where God has brought us from. Don't forget where you came from.

Sin is sin. Don't go around approving certain sins in your life or others' lives. Stand up for what's right.

Day 221

Today encourage someone. God surrounded you with loving and encouraging people, so make sure you do the same for others now that you're stronger.

Day 222

Your burdens may be heavy, and you might feel like life is too much to handle. The burden was never for you to carry. Today, give it all to God. Let go and let God handle it. The battle is not yours. It's the Lord's.

Day 223

You don't have to know how, when, and where. You just have to trust God & have faith. We go through life facing challenges and problems so we can GROW spiritually. It's all part of the process. Keep the FAITH.

Day 224

Who are you surrounding yourself with? You need positive, motivating, and spiritual people in your life. If you're receiving advice, make sure the individual giving it is living a positive and spiritual life. Don't listen to someone that has never been through something, but they always giving advice.

Day 225

If God wanted you dead for sinning, He would have killed you a long time ago. Don't keep going back to that place doing the same thing after God saved & delivered you from that sin.

Day 226

Today your situation might be one way, but God can change it in a second, minute, hour, or day. Don't look at what it looks like, but now God is going to make a way. Say, "Lord I don't know how, when, or where, but I trust you. I know you're going to bring me out." Continue to pray and watch God move on your behalf.

Day 227

You may feel like at your current age you should have accomplished or have much more in life, but don't let age put a dictation on your life. When God says it's time, that's when it will happen. Everything has a time and reason. Be patient. It will come. Just keep praying.

Day 228

You're walking around complaining about what you don't have, and there are people that don't have a life. They're dead, but as long as you're alive you are blessed. You have the greatest gift, and that's your LIFE. Stop complaining because there are people that have it worse than you.

Day 229

Stop allowing your feelings to get in the way of your personal journey & growth. Your feelings & emotions can only get you so far. Take action and stop looking for someone to feel sorry for you.

Day 230

Walk with confidence. You're a King's kid. If you want it speak it into existence. Name it and claim it daily. There's nothing God can't and won't do for you.

Day 231

When people put you down, just know God will always push you up. Stay encouraged. You can do anything you put your mind to.

Day 232

We all have an assignment for our life, but what will we do during our lifetime? When we die there's a beginning and end date on our tomb stone. What will the hyphen between the begin date and end date tell about you? What impact have you left on society?

Day 233

Men and women: don't rent your body out when it doesn't belong to you. Your body is a holy temple and it belongs to the Lord.

Day 234

Whose approval are you waiting for? If God said it… It can be done. You don't need approval from man.

Day 235

No one knows your story, but through your conversations the truth is expressed. Everyone won't listen because they're too busy telling their own stories. How will they know you're crying out for help? Make sure you're slow to speak and quick to listen when someone is sharing their story. By listening, you might get a glimpse of the person behind the mask.

Day 236

Stop reading into things. God is trying to bless you, but you're too busy trying to figure God out and asking Him if He's sure. Are you serious? Of course, He's sure.

Day 237

You might find yourself doing something that you have no idea how it's going to come together. You act on it and keep doing it. What you don't understand is it's a set-up by God. You can't find the purpose behind your actions, but God knows He's setting everything up. Don't stop! Keep going and believing because something great is about to take place.

Day 238

Your frustration doesn't solve anything. Stop what you're doing and start back once you're calm.

Day 239

Just because you're feeling lonely doesn't mean you find a mate or a relationship to fill your void. Stop accepting anything just to have something.

Jumping into another relationship or marriage doesn't heal you from your last relationship or marriage.

Day 241

Get up and don't look back. God has allowed you to see a new day. It's not too late to make a change and difference.

Day 242

We all have been sold something in life we couldn't use or was worthless, but Jesus is free, and we can use Him every day and every hour. Let's invest in something that's worth having and mandatory.

Sometimes we need to start over again and again until we get it right. Don't give up until you get it right.

Speak it into existence. You don't have to see it to believe it and speak it.

Day 245

One might talk about what you did or didn't do, but no one can tear down what you established or proved. Evidence and facts tell the truth.

Day 246

If everything feels like it's at a standstill, continue to be still. Change will come soon.

No one is perfect, but you should strive to be the best version of you.

Day 248

A lot of people, businesses, and organizations can sell you a dream where the executive team only benefits from it, but God has an investment where everyone benefits, and you can be rich holistically.

Day 249

Make sure our kids know their history. It's important they know their past and present as they prepare for their future.

Day 250

Don't wait for man to acknowledge, support, and encourage you. There's motivation, determination, and a fight within you. Make sure you apply it to your life.

Day 251

Positive energy makes a difference in your life. If it's not positive, don't entertain it. Positive energy not only makes a difference in your life, but in the lives of those around you. Surround yourself with positivity – don't entertain negativity.

Don't make promises you can't keep because it can cost you greatly.

There's a difference between being nice and firm. You can be nice and mean what you say.

Take it one day at a time. Day by day. Stand firm and hold on. No matter what, don't give in and bend.

Day 255

If money, materialistic things, and a mate made you complete, you wouldn't need God. Make sure your void is filled with Godly things.

The sun won't shine every day, but you can't allow it to determine how you respond to your day.

Day 257

Love is profound, and it has to be demonstrated in life. If one lacks love, how can he or she live or love their own life? In order to understand love, you must experience and understand God's love and your love for yourself first.

Day 258

Why complain when you know you haven't done anything to fix the problem? Complaining is never the solution. It's just the verb in a problem.

Day 259

Being content is being in a state of acceptance and satisfaction.

Day 260

Don't be surprised. Be aware and accepting of the expected and unexpected. Make sure you accept what you can and can't change.

Day 261

Yes! God sees all things, and our title doesn't give us an exception to the rule. Let's do what's right. Even when no one is looking.

Day 262

Life is what you make it. If you're not happy it's because you decided not to be. Do something about it.

Day 263

Keep living! You'll find out what's important and what's not important. One day your priorities will change.

Day 264

Your vision is only limited when you don't pursue your dream.

Day 265

It's ok to look up to people and become motivated through them but stop praising them and all their accomplishments. Your praise of their accomplishments can distract you from your goals. You too busy running around supporting and doing for others; therefore, you neglect your vision, goals, and the calling God has over your life.

Don't let your environment get you off track.
Learn to adapt in any environment.

Day 267

Silence is the best answer when you don't want to say the wrong thing or when you don't know what to say.

Day 268

Don't go into debt trying to entertain others in life. Make sure you only manage the things you can afford.

Day 269

We don't have to see it, but we do have to believe it. You might not know what, when, or where, but trust God for all the details. Anticipate great things daily.

Day 270

You don't have to get married, win the lotto, have a baby, buy a house or car, get a new job, get a raise, go out with friends, celebrate a life event, but when you go to church one way, and don't leave there the same. That's a great feeling. Cast all your cares on the Lord. It's nothing like having joy, peace, and love from the Lord.

Day 271

Don't keep starving yourself because you're afraid to eat at the table in that particular environment. Every environment brings about change and opportunities. We must be willing to seek opportunities in any situation.

Day 272

We shouldn't be doing the same thing over and over again every year. Try something different especially if what you have done for years hasn't worked.

No matter what it looks like or feels like, you get up and you grind.

Day 274

Do you find yourself fighting the Lord? You might not notice it, but He's trying to take the wheel and take you to the next level in your life. You're too busy trying to control your own destination. Stop fighting, let the wheel go, and let God be your pilot.

Day 275

When you know your purpose, the reward is beyond money. Your passion becomes your motivation not money.

If you want to accomplish your goals in life
you can't be afraid to fail.

Day 277

At some point, we all have been guilty of showing off our accomplishments, life events, or celebrations, but what people don't see is the debt we've accumulated & the bills that didn't get paid. Don't let what your neighbor gets - get you off track. You may be seeing an illusion.

Day 278

If it wasn't for the Lord, you wouldn't be in your current situation. Praise Him because He didn't have to do it. God has been so good to us, and we need to tell & show Him we're thankful.

Day 279

Mom, dad, or a leader might think they're fixing things and hiding sins, but God knows and sees all things. We still have to stand before God on judgment day, and our parents can't get us in heaven. Embarrassment, humiliation, and pain is all part of our growth.

Day 280

Your faith & experience in the Lord will keep you going. Don't stop believing.

Day 281

You never had full control of your life, but God gave us a free will. So, you can make the decision day-to-day to do the right thing. No excuses.

Day 282

Thank God for change. You will see things totally different. Don't be afraid of change.

Day 283

There's a level of respect each individual should give one another no matter what.

Day 284

When you know your purpose in life the reward is beyond money. Your passion becomes your motivation not money.

Day 285

When you're done chasing money, sex, cars, houses, a spouse, attention, fame, love, drugs, alcohol, parties, harm, the life you want, and other people's dreams, you will have no choice but to chase God. Don't let it be too late while playing in the fire. Tomorrow isn't promised, and you might get burned while playing.

Day 286

God was working things out for your good last year, and you had no idea it was tied or linked together. In every season, God always work things out for our good in the bad. Don't be afraid.

Everything has a time & place, and during the process everything will come together.

You don't have to be perfect for God to use you. He accepts you, and then He turns around and mends you.

Day 289

Just because you don't know which direction to go doesn't mean you turn around and go back. Keep going – Let the Lord be your guide.

Day 290

Your now doesn't determine your future. God specializes in making things that look bad look good. Trust Him! Look at yourself and your life.

Day 291

Some of us chasing degrees until we learn better. Some people focused on obtaining degrees, but not allowing God to use them through the degrees. It's a great accomplishment to have a degree, but if you aren't using your degree(s) to follow God's plan for your life, then your degree is worthless.

Our past decisions can affect our future, but our past decisions don't determine our future.

Make time for the things and people that are important.

Day 294

No one should have to tell you what's right or wrong. You might have some influencers, but daily you decide if you're going to do what's right or wrong. You make your own decisions, but it's timeout for making the wrong decisions.

Day 295

You must admit it, since some people left out of your life, it has been so peaceful, calm, and stress-free. You should thank them. You wanted to hold on to some people, but they were not meant to stay in your life. Aren't you glad you let go and let God take control?

You're entitled to have the same things or much more than the next man. The favor of God rests upon your life. God made you, and you're important.

Day 297

Think about it - how many times have you gone through something and God didn't make a way for you? Everything always works out. Our past and now may say, "NO", but our future and God is saying, "YES." Trust Him.

What the heart and mind want might not be what the heart and mind need. Do you really need what you want?

Day 299

Everybody is not willing to go the extra mile for you. What you do for others they won't do for you. Your expectation level is higher. Just because you go above and beyond for others, doesn't mean the next person will do the same.

Day 300

Being blessed, prosperous, and rich can all be misunderstood. Most of the time man associates these three things with money and material possessions, and somehow holistically and spirituality are missed.

Day 301

When you're busy taking care of your own business, you don't have time to keep up with someone else's business. Keep your eyes on the prize, and don't worry about others.

Day 302

You aren't weak-therefore don't act weak. Only the strong survives and win. Whatever you speak and display that's what it will be. Remain strong, and don't give in.

Regardless, with you or without you, life goes on. Life and time don't stop just for you.

Day 304

Even when you're exhausted, keep going. There's work to be done. Don't give up! You might be overwhelmed with a full plate in life. Make sure to clean your plate and wash it before you get another one.

Day 305

When you learn to live within your means, you work to make a living not just to pay bills. Once you have experienced it or when you're wiser, you don't make decisions just to satisfy your taste, but you make decisions to satisfy your necessities and priorities.

Day 306

You will be able to identify your true family and friends. They will deal with you, love you, be true, do for you, check on you, include you, pray for you, and respect you.

Day 307

Behaviors are learned or taught. Don't assume the actions you're witnessing developed overnight. Sometimes we think we are born a certain way. Your genetic makeup accounts for some of your actions, but the majority of your actions/behaviors are related to how you were taught to respond or act accordingly.

Just because you were taught something doesn't mean you can't break the cycle. Some behaviors should never be taught.

Day 308

Success is not defined by what type of car you drive, what type of house you own, how much money you have, how many buildings or businesses you own, what kind of degree you hold, or how many people you know. Some people define success this way, but there are many people with all these things and they're still not happy. Success and happiness are in the eye of the beholder not the individual. Your definition of success could mean you're miserable. You need substance because tangible things can only take you so far in life. Try Jesus because He works miracles and He lasts forever.

Day 309

You only get one life to live. Include God in your life and make the best of it. You can live, love, and laugh, but you must make sure God is the author of your life.

Day 310

People will say a lot of things about you - good and bad. It doesn't matter what they say, but it does matter how you react to what they say. You won't be everyone's favorite, everyone won't agree with you, everyone won't like you, and everyone won't care to hear what you have to say or do. Just know that you must take the punches and roll with them. Make sure you stay in your character because people are waiting for you to act out. Some individuals like mess, and they want to see you act like them. You can tell a person who you are, but your actions tell them who you really are.

Day 311

When things don't go as planned, improvise. Don't sit idle, do something. When things go wrong you might not be able to fix things, but you can improvise.

Day 312

Things don't become a problem in your life until it becomes your problem and you're experiencing it. When people go through trials, you can relate to them knowing how they feel because you're going through it or been through it.

Day 313

Get up and keep going. Don't allow the yesterday or yesteryear keep you from going forward. Adversity will come, but you can and will overcome it. Keep going and defeat your adversities.

Day 314

Your life has been spared for a reason. Make sure you understand and know why. It's not by coincidence that you're still here. God has a plan and purpose for your life. Give thanks and walk into your purpose.

Day 315

We may plan our day or our life out, but when God interrupts our plans we must understand, we're on His time not our time. You may try to plan your life out, but God is in control. He will twist and flip your life around, but it's for your good. So, just endure the process.

Sometimes it's best to say nothing. Just watch and learn a lot. Be slow to speak and quick to listen & watch.

Day 317

Make sure you hold everyone accountable for their actions and not just a select few. Stop allowing certain people to get away with doing the wrong thing in your life. Don't make an excuse for a few, then hold others accountable. Right is right and wrong is wrong. When you see it call it like it is.

Day 318

Your struggles, setbacks, and disappointments are not always about you. Sometimes it's for someone else. Your testimony assists others with their breakthrough, deliverance, and encouragement. God knows what you can and can't handle. He knows you will be a living testimony to many through your struggles.

Have you ever found yourself assisting someone going through a test in life because you been there and done that? God will put you through it so you can bring others through it. Stay in the race and don't give up because someone out there needs you and they're depending on you to get through it. Remain faithful! Helping others isn't about you; it's about them.

Day 319

Our choices affect our life, but they don't affect our future, unless we allow them to. You're going to make good and bad choices in life, but you don't have to let your choices determine your future.

Day 320

Make time for those that make time for you. Stop paying attention to those that are not paying attention to you. You're not their priority. So, stop making them yours.

Day 321

You can't control another's actions, but you can control your own. Stop trying to fix others when you haven't been fixed yourself. Control your own life and environment. Work on you!

Day 322

Don't allow your circumstances to keep you down but allow it to change you and make a difference in your life. Let your life impact others in a positive way. Everything happens for a reason. Make sure you pay attention and understand why. When something bad happens, God will turn it around for your good or for the good of others.

Day 323

When we don't understand God does. Pray to the Lord and trust Him no matter what. Some of our greatest and most difficult tasks come from the Lord. Sometimes we don't understand why, but the Lord knows why. During the storm, multiple lives will be saved. Stand firm and stay strong. Hold on because there's a blessing behind all things. For God gets the glory.

Day 324

Good things come to those that wait. Just be patient.

Day 325

The road untraveled is unseen and unknown - don't let the fear of the unknown keep you from going ahead. Don't be afraid to accept life challenges because you have no idea what the outcome will be.

Day 326

Be a blessing to others. What will you do today to bless someone else? It's not all about you, you, and you. Are your intentions pure?

Day 327

Everybody doesn't have to like you nor approve of you. As long as, you like and approve of. That's all you need. "Get your life back."

Don't worry, God will not allow you to lack for anything. Try Him and see.

Day 329

All things must come to an end, make every event in your life is to be rememberable. Some events we want to forget but, remember them all so you can remind yourself where you came from. Remind yourself how good God has been to you. Love God, serve God, live and love life.

Day 330

Some find it difficult to follow directions, but only if you know how much time you could save by following instructions, directions in life. Our way is not always the right way. So, make sure you have guidance in your life. God will never mislead you. Try Him and see.

Day 331

Don't attempt to please people. You will find yourself confused, disappointed, and hurt. Please God. Be blessed, be thankful, be proud of yourself, motivate yourself, encourage yourself, love yourself, and stand up for yourself. Stop allowing people to make you feel less than others. We are all God's children, and He loves us. You're entitled to everything. God has a plan for us. You're an heir and the King's kid. Smile and hold your head high. You're from a royal bloodline.

Day 332

You don't have to compete with others. We all have something that someone else doesn't have. God made every one of us, and we are all unique and wonderfully made. Stop looking at your fellow next man for comparison. We are all BLESSED! Look back over your life and be thankful for your now, past, and future. God has been good to you. You can't measure your outcome with someone else's life. When you see others doing good celebrate with them. God made something special about each one of us. Stop comparing yourself!

Even when you don't get a response, keep replying and responding. Do your part and let God do the rest.

Some things you can't change. Stop trying to change everybody and everything.

Day 335

In order to get the best in life, you have to work hard. Therefore, to whom much is given much is required. Nothing worth having comes easy. Stop asking for things you're not willing to work hard to obtain.

Day 336

If you take on a job or task, make sure you do it right. If you're not going to do it right don't do it at all.

Day 337

Being bitter won't change anything nor will it solve your problems. So, let's find strength, peace, hope, and happiness in the Lord. He can change all things. Stop walking around sour and mad. Get your joy, peace, and love back. You can find it all within the Lord.

Day 338

Rejoice and be glad even when everything is going or goes wrong. It's only temporary. Trouble doesn't last forever. Be thankful in the midst of the good and bad.

Day 339

God protects us when we don't even protect ourselves. So many times, we play with fire, and we should have gotten burned, but God preserves and protects us. This is another reason to thank and praise Him daily.

Day 340

No one wants to repeat the same test again and again and continue to fail, but at some point, our failures become our greatest accomplishments and success. Even I have felt like a failure, but I know that my failures have led me to my greatest accomplishments. We must fight and continue to make a difference in the midst of our failures and disappointments. We are our best advocate.

Day 341

Just because you can beat the system, take shortcuts, and always getting things at a discounted rate doesn't make it right. Everything free is not good and right. Stop looking for something free and easy. Get up and work for things you desire. Only then will you appreciate the real value of things. Anything worth having is worth working hard for.

Day 342

I've learned that just because someone's best didn't match everyone else's best, doesn't mean that individual didn't do his or her best. Everybody is on different levels; therefore, we must be thankful for the effort and progress made. So often our expectations are set on the limits of others, and what we normally see others do or perform. My norm may not be your norm, your norm may not be my norm. Your best won't be everybody else's best and vice versa. Everyone is not on the same level as you. Stop expecting their best to be your best. Stay in your own lane.

Day 343

Continue to be slow to speak, but quick to listen. You don't want to miss anything. Don't talk too much that you forget to listen. How can we get our instructions and understanding if we're always talking?

Face your fears or enemy is to face them head on. Stand strong! Face your fears and your enemies. God is in control.

Day 345

While you're waiting on others to make a difference in your life, why don't you make a difference in someone else's life? It's not always about you. Bless someone and stop looking for someone to do something for you all the time. Do something different from what you've been doing.

Day 346

You only need one, two, or three to stand in agreement with you. You don't need an entourage, a lot of friends, or crowd to support you. You need God and a few to stand in agreement and tell you what's right. Stop looking for people to validate you when they're not authorized to do so.

Day 347

Everyone won't understand what you do, but it's ok because it wasn't assigned to everybody. That's why God trusted you because He knew you would get it done. Its ok, your assignment isn't everybody else's assignment. You might be crawling, walking, or running, but people won't be going the same pace as you.

Day 348

No one knows what tomorrow holds, but each of us should have great expectations daily. Don't give up! Expect the best and don't expect anything less. You deserve to have the best. Speak it into existence and don't give up until you get what you want.

Day 349

There are more people wanting to be friends versus being in a committed relationship or marriage. We all have plenty of friends and some have too many. At some point, you'll do the right thing and grow up. If you don't you can forever remain a friend to someone.
Don't accept too many of friendships and miss the relationship. Everybody doesn't want to do right. Make sure you know your friends' purpose in your life.

Day 350

Even when you mess up, continue to strive to get it right. Ask God to forgive you and keep moving forward. No, you won't continue to get chance after chance, but God's grace and mercy allows us to get it right. Don't continue to live in sin.

Day 351

You never know what God is setting you up for. Be patient and thankful. Everything will work itself out. Go with the flow and be patient.

Day 352

We must encourage one another in the midst of turmoil. Don't sit and watch your brother and sister sink or fail. Give a helping hand and pray with them. Stop waiting for others to fail. If you can't help, pray, or say something good, don't say anything at all.

Day 353

Every day won't be a good day but make the best out of it. Your decisions determine the outcome.

Day 354

There are so many things we want to say, but don't say anything. Silence is sometimes the best treatment. Let it go. Sometimes a million words are not worth anything. Don't let quantity confuse your quality.

Day 355

Don't stop being you. God made you different for a reason. We all have a different calling, assignment, and mission. We're just trying to accomplish our goals. Don't try to change what God created within you.

Day 356

Tie up all loose ends before going into something new. If you don't tie things up, things will unravel. Don't go around leaving things untied. Take care of your business or someone else will.

Day 357

Today is a new day. "Repent" and don't go back into those places that caused you to sin. Our God is a forgiving God, just because He forgives doesn't mean you can keep doing wrong. It's His grace and mercy that keeps us. Don't take advantage of God's grace and mercy.

Day 358

Don't let anyone determine how your day goes. Don't allow any negativism in your space.

Day 359

Nobody knows your story like you. Therefore, everybody won't understand your actions, but it's ok because it's only for you and not everybody else. Don't expect anyone to understand you, but God. That's why you're different.

Day 360

You can't expect everything to happen overnight. Everything goes through a process. Don't rush it. Be patient and know God is in control. It's going to happen if it is supposed to happen. In due time everything will work out. Be patient.

Day 361

When you're off to yourself and in isolation is when you truly begin to learn yourself. You begin to see things differently and you see things and people for who they really are. You must admit, since you let some people go, you have been stress-free, and you can hear and see clearer. The drama doesn't exist, and you feel free. Don't allow people or things to keep you from being free with a peaceful mind. We need isolation from others, but we feel like we need an entourage to make it in life. Your family, friends, entourage, and associates can't get you into heaven. They might influence you to go to heaven or hell, but they can't get you there. Only you can determine your eternal outcome.

Day 362

So many times we ask for something, but when we get it we don't do anything with it. What are you going to do when you get it? Stop asking for things you can't handle. Just because it looks good, sounds good, or feels good doesn't mean it's good. We tend to chase a dream or want what God never intended for us to have. We become impatient, discontent, and anxious; therefore, we settle for doing all the work trying to keep something together that was never meant to stay or be together.

If we all had it together and if we all were perfect nobody would need God, but we can't live without Him (God).

Even if everything appears to be falling apart just keep going no matter what.

Day 365

You're the head and not the tail. You're blessed and highly favored. No weapon formed against you shall prosper. You're blessed going in and coming out. You lack nothing. You have more than enough. Your life is filled with peace, love, joy, and happiness. You're the lender and not the borrower. You can have whatever you want and need through your father. You're bold, wise, knowledgeable, courageous, faithful, and strong. You're healthy and wealthy holistically.

Your family, friends, enemies, and connections are all blessed. People will see the CHRIST within you, and his light will always shine through you. You won't settle for less only for God's best. You will not confirm to the things of this world. You're qualified! You're the chosen one. You will trust God and not man. You will travel this world and bless many. God is raising up sons and daughters that's not afraid to tell people everywhere they go about his goodness. Know who you are, and know your purpose. You're more than a conqueror. You're a Kings kid. All you have to do is call and cry out Abby to your father. People will know you by your fruits and spirit everywhere you go.

About the Author

Sequoya Trimble is an inspirational woman of God and that loves motivating and inspiring people. This is one of many of her inspirational books to come. She has a passion to help others, and always willing to share her knowledge, testimonies, and life experiences which assist others with growth. She's been a registered nurse for going on eighteen years and enjoys providing care holistically. One of her goals is speaking life into people and reminding them daily they can make it no matter what. Sequoya has over 5000 followers on social media, and family, friends, and strangers love seeking advice and receiving inspirational words from her. She's always positive, full of life, and encouraging others to remain positive. There's nothing like having positive energy and a beautiful smile in your space which she demonstrates daily. She works and live in Memphis, Tennessee with her son.